S0-CGQ-017

Massachusetts

MASSACHUSETTS
From the Berkshires to the Cape

Nancy Sirkis
Text by Walter Muir Whitehill

A Studio Book · The Viking Press · New York

Other books by Nancy Sirkis

Newport: *Pleasures and Palaces*
Boston
One Family
Reflections of 1776: *The Colonies Revisited*

First published in 1977 by The Viking Press
625 Madison Avenue, New York, N.Y. 10022
Published simultaneously in Canada by
Penguin Books Canada Limited

Library of Congress Cataloging in Publication Data
Sirkis, Nancy.
Massachusetts: from the Berkshires to the Cape.
(A Studio book)
1. Historic buildings–Massachusetts–Conservation and restoration. 2. Massachusetts–Description and travel–1951– I. Whitehill, Walter Muir, 1905–
F65.S54 069'.53 77-22404
ISBN 0-670-46123-7

Printed in the United States of America

Title page: Crane's Beach, Ipswich.

Contents

To Andrew and Daniel

Preface

One of the smallest states, Massachusetts is nonetheless uncommonly diverse in character. For one, it is most generously endowed with a great variety of landscape: the Berkshire Mountains in the west; the flat farm country at its center; the eastern sea coast with large cities, two capes, and an assortment of islands.

The more I photographed the landscape, the more I grew to love the land. There is something so gentle and, at the same time, awe-inspiring about waiting in the damp early morning cold for the fog to lift and reveal mountains, grazing cows, silhouettes of trees on isolated country roads, and small houses dotting the rolling countryside.

As I moved east, I was fascinated by the furrows of the farmlands, but especially with the dramatic change in patterns on the land as one season gave way to the next. The closer I approached the coast, the more intrusive became the cities that seemed to be ever crowding one another. Mill towns, such as Lowell, Lawrence, and Haverhill, offer a bleak contrast to the surrounding landscape; modern architecture in Boston, Worcester, and Springfield creates geometric patterns out of concrete, glass, and steel.

Cape Ann and Cape Cod offer a glimpse of yet another world. Desolate marshland, endless, monumental untouched sand dunes, small streets in fishing towns, and the jagged primeval coastline contrast harshly with the cheap commercial enterprises that appear on the swarming streets of Rockport or Provincetown.

I hope the reader will enjoy taking this brief, one-hundred-and-ninety-mile journey with me through mountains, farms, cities, and coastal areas. And I hope my camera's work has done justice to the beauty of this unusual state.

NANCY SIRKIS

The State House.

∧ On the campus of Smith College, Northampton. > Dennis, Cape Cod.

< In the Berkshires. ∧ Sand dunes, Provincetown, Cape Cod.

>> View from West Gloucester looking toward Crane's Beach, Ipswich.

Oak Bluffs, Martha's Vineyard.

Massachusetts

COLONIAL
LANTERN

Preservation of the Landscape

Although Massachusetts is not a large state, it comprises an extraordinary variety of landscapes that have raised the spirits of some of its inhabitants. The Puritan settlers of the Massachusetts Bay Company in the seventeenth century were not oblivious of their surroundings. Witness the following passage by the Boston judge Samuel Sewall, from his *Phaenomena Quaedam Apocalyptica ad Aspectum Novi Orbis Configurata, or, Some Few Lines Towards a Description of the New Heaven as it Makes to Those Who Stand upon the New Earth*, published in 1697.

> As long as Plum Island shall faithfully keep the Commanded Post; Notwithstanding the hectoring words and hard Blows of the proud and boisterous Ocean; As long as any Salmon, or Sturgeon shall swim in the streams of the Merrimack; or any Perch or Pickeril in Crane Pond; As long as the Sea Fowl shall know the Time of their Coming, and not neglect seasonally to visit the Places of their Acquaintance; As long as any Cattel shall be fed with the Grass growing in the meadows, which do humbly bow themselves before Turkie Hill; As long as any Sheep shall walk upon Old Town Hills, and shall from thence pleasantly look down upon the River Parker, and the fruitful Marishes lying beneath; As long as any free and harmless Doves shall find a White Oak or other Tree within the Township to perch, or feed, or build a careless Nest upon; and shall voluntarily present themselves to perform the office of Gleaners after Barley-Harvest; As long as Nature shall not grow old and dote; but shall constantly remember to give the rows of

Newburyport.

> Indian Corn their education by Pairs; So long shall Christians be born there; and being first made meet, shall from thence be Translated to be made partakers of the Inheritance of the Saints in Light.

These lines recall images from his childhood in the town of Newbury in Essex County, to which Sewall, born in England in 1652, had been taken by his parents at the age of nine. The places that he evokes are impressed in my memory from frequent visits with my friend Elliott Perkins, who has a house on Hay Street in Newbury from which one sees Old Town Hill, rising above the "fruitful Marishes."

Irrelevant bits of historical continuity often pop up parenthetically into my mind. Whenever I think of Judge Sewall it amuses me to remember that he was the first treasurer of the Trustees of the Charity of Edward Hopkins (from 1713 to 1717), a not very onerous office that I have held since 1958. This body, which I suspect is the oldest continuously surviving charity in Massachusetts, annually provides scholarships in divinity and awards prize books—called "Deturs"—to meritorious undergraduates in Harvard Unversity and also offers classical prizes and scholarships to students in the Cambridge High and Latin School from funds bequeathed by Edward Hopkins, a governor of the Connecticut Colony, who died in 1657. Lowell House, Harvard University, of which Elliott Perkins was master from 1940 to 1963, was named in honor of a family that settled in 1639 at Newbury, within sight of Old Town Hill. My granddaughter, Diana Randolph Laing of the class of 1979—the eleventh Harvard generation since the Reverend John Wilson of the class of 1642—lives in Lowell House, of which my father-in-law, Professor Julian Lowell Coolidge, was master from 1930 to 1940; where I was Elliott Perkins's senior tutor from 1952 to 1956; and where my son-in-law and Diana's father, C. Christopher Laing, class of 1953, lived as an undergraduate.

I was born in Cambridge on September 28, 1905, almost within sound of the Harvard College bell, and have lived in Massachusetts for more than sixty of my seventy-two years. Studies in Spanish Romanesque architecture, which I began as a Harvard undergraduate, kept me in Europe for an extended period. In 1936 I settled on the

Common at North Andover, and there I have been ever since, save for four years at the Navy Department during World War II. Only in North Andover did I crawl sufficiently out of the middle ages to discover that my native state was of remarkable interest. In the preface to *Boston: A Topographical History*, first published in 1959, I explained my change of heart:

> For twenty-five years I took New England in general, and Boston and Cambridge in particular, for granted, without strong emotion for or against. It was only in 1935, when I returned from five unbroken years in Europe, that I looked at them with the slightest interest. During those five years I had been studying and photographing Romanesque architecture in Spain. In that relatively thinly populated and unindustrialized country, which I loved, I had come to see something of the influence of geography and topography upon the settlement, planning and growth of towns and cities. With a small Spanish town, free of sprawling suburbs, it is easy to see the relation between sites and buildings and the importance of rivers—in short to begin to understand why someone first considered a given spot useful for settlement, and how, from that beginning, churches, mills, markets, and houses had been placed where they were. As I looked at New England with eyes fresh from a long absence, I found a wholly new amusement in trying to fathom the archaeological and topographical reasons why my childhood surroundings had become what they were rather than something else. In the end I became so absorbed in this, and related games, that New England history has become my chief interest.

A few months after settling in North Andover, I joined the staff of the Peabody Museum of Salem, where I spent six happy years. This is the oldest museum in continuous operation in the United States, having been founded in 1799 by shipmasters of the East India Marine Society. It has three specialties: maritime history, the ethnology of the Pacific and Japan, and the natural history of Essex County. It was a pleasant half hour's drive from my house to the museum. Forty years ago a relatively uncrowded Route 114 ran through rolling farming country in North Andover and Middleton and through rich market gardens on the edge of Danvers before reaching the urban precincts of Salem, once a seaport but later industrialized.

Although the great days of shipping were a century in the past, many of the fine houses built by shipmasters and merchants still lent distinction to the older parts of Salem, Marblehead, and Newburyport. Gloucester harbor, however, was still alive with fishing vessels, while coasting schooners, with unglamorous cargoes of coal or lumber, still occasionally entered these Essex County ports. In the James and Story shipyards of Essex, wooden fishing vessels still continued to be built and launched into a river so narrow that it seemed incredible that the ships could make their way to the open sea. There at Essex one could still see the traditional processes of shipbuilding, much as they had gone on since the seventeenth century, when the settlers of Massachusetts—from necessity rather than choice, like Norwegians in similar circumstances—had turned to the sea for their livelihood. Otherwise there was more to be learned about maritime history within the walls of the Peabody Museum than by wandering around Essex County waterfronts.

Various museum errands took me to many neighboring towns in Essex County. For the sheer joy of exploration, I often lengthened my journey between Salem and North Andover. So many pleasant country roads seemed worth revisiting that before long I knew my way around Essex County fairly thoroughly. The variety of landscape within a few miles of North Andover was extraordinary. In some central states, one can travel for hours without encountering significant change, but here the mood easily altered in a short time.

The Merrimac River, which flowed down from New Hampshire, skirted North Andover after providing water power for the industrial cities of Lowell and Lawrence. Between Haverhill and Newburyport, where the Merrimac flows into the sea, its valley was serene and bucolic, even though its waters had become unhealthy for man or fish. East of Haverhill the farm where the Quaker poet John Greenleaf Whittier was born in 1807 still looked as it did when he described it in "Snowbound." The Merrimac at Groveland, Rocks Village, Merrimacport, or Salisbury Point, was still uncommonly beautiful.

Whittier had a deep affection for this valley and for Essex County in general. He was, indeed, so taken by Judge Sewall's description of Newbury that in 1859 he turned it into verse, with somewhat unfortunate results. The opening lines will indicate the extent to which seventeenth-century prose may be more poetic than nineteenth-century rhymes.

> As long as Plum Island, to guard the coast
> As God appointed; shall keep its post;
> As long as a salmon shall haunt the deep
> of Merrimac River, or sturgeon leap;
> As long as the annual sea-fowl know
> Their time to come and their time to go.

The Merrimac enters the sea through a narrow opening between two sandy bars: Salisbury Beach to the north and Plum Island to the south. The latter, about eight miles long and a half a mile wide, at the most, extends from Newburyport to Ipswich; it is a favorite spot for bird-watchers. Behind it lies a great area of salt marshes, through which the Parker and Plum Island Rivers, and smaller streams, meander. Beyond the opening through which they reach the sea begins Castle Neck in Ipswich, a superlative sandy beach, backed by ever-changing dunes. This area was the inspiration of the physician ornithologist Charles Wendell Townsend, whose books *Sand Dunes and Salt Marshes* and *Beach Grass* are the ideal guides to the region. Behind the dunes are still more marshes; to the east is the Atlantic-bound Essex River, by which Essex-built vessels reached the sea.

Within a few miles of this protean landscape, the rocky peninsula of Cape Ann juts into the ocean, with steep cliffs and granite quarries. Rockport, now a nest of artists, has a granite breakwater, begun with the thought that Sandy Bay might become a naval anchorage. Annisquam has its share of both summer residents and year-round lobstermen. Leaving Cape Ann and going southwest along the coast, one reaches Salem by way of Manchester Beverly Farms, Prides Crossing, and Beverly. This "North Shore," originally a region of poor farms and rocky seaside pastures, was transformed in the second half of the nineteenth century into a region of large summer estates. The evergreens and rhododendrons planted around some of the houses a century ago have grown to such magnificence as to obscure the woebegone quality of the original landscape.

Rocky peninsulas give variety to the coast. Marblehead is a picturesque port with seamen's and merchants' houses tucked between outcroppings of ledge. Nahant, connected with Swampscott and Lynn by a causeway, became a favorite summer resort for nineteenth-century Bostonians. All this variety of landscape was available in less than an hour's drive from North Andover, not to mention the pleasures of inland towns like Topsfield, Boxford, and West Newbury, with their share of hills, winding streams, and ponds. Such variety leads residents of Essex County to consider their natural surroundings the most attractive in the state, but the truth is that here are few really dull and monotonous areas in Massachusetts.

John S. Driscoll of the *Boston Globe*, describing the state in the fifteenth edition of the *Encyclopaedia Britannica*, observes:

> A walk along the Massachusetts coast would register about 1,500 miles, yet the cross-country distances are only 190 miles from east to west and 110 miles north to south. The jagged coast winds from Rhode Island around Cape Cod, in and out of scenic harbors along the south shore of Boston, through Boston Harbor and up the North Shore, finally swinging around the painters' paradise of Cape Ann before reaching New Hampshire.

This jagged coast, like most physical features of Massachusetts, is a legacy from the Ice Age, when glaciers were scouring out bays and inlets and littering the land with debris that formed numerous smooth-sloped hills, known as drumlins.

Henry D. Thoreau likened Cape Cod to

> the bared and bended arm of Massachusetts; the shoulder is at Buzzard's Bay; the elbow, or crazy-bone, at Cape Mallebarre; the wrist at Truro; and the sandy fist at Provincetown,—behind which the State stands on her guard, with her back to the Green Mountains, and her feet planted on the shore of the ocean, like an athlete

protecting her Bay,—boxing with northeast storms, and ever and anon, heaving up her Atlantic adversary from the lap of earth,—ready to thrust forward her other fist, which keeps guard the while upon her breast at Cape Ann.

Seventy years later Samuel Eliot Morison called the two capes "the horns of Massachusetts Bay; two giant limbs thrown seaward, like the wings of a fish-weir, to guide seaborne commerce into Boston's fruitful embrace." At the head of the bay created by these great protecting-welcoming arms was the hilly Shawmut peninsula, upon which Boston was settled in 1630. As early as 1634, in a promotional tract entitled *New England Prospects*, William Wood described the place as "fittest for such as can trade into England." For more than two centuries Boston was primarily a seaport. Today, when the ships have gone, its Logan International Airport is nearer Europe than any other airport in the United States.

Unlike New York City, where the Hudson River provided easy communication with upstate regions, Boston had no comparable waterway. The Charles and Mystic Rivers, which flow into Boston harbor, are modest meandering streams of no consequence to travelers. Central Massachusetts is pleasantly rolling country, veined by numerous small streams and ponds, some of which have been dammed to create reservoirs. The most conspicuous feature in this part is Mount Wachusett (2006 feet). The noblest river of the state, the Connecticut, flows north and south, some eighty miles west of Boston. Its broad valley is both fertile and beautiful. Farther west are the Berkshire Hills, a segment of the Appalachian mountain chain. Mount Greylock (3491 feet), in the Berkshires, is the highest point in Massachusetts.

The Creator, using glaciers as a sculptor's tool, achieved remarkable natural beauty and variety in Massachusetts, as the photographs in this book show. But man, especially American man, has an aptitude for damaging his surroundings. If "free enterprise" had had its way, there would be fewer good subjects to photograph. It is largely due to a small group of Bostonians at the end of the last century that many of the most dramatic and beautiful features of the landscape have survived.

The nineteenth century was a period of extraordinary change in Boston. In 1800 the town was a homogeneous English seaport with 25,000 inhabitants; in 1900 it was a polyglot city of over half a million, nine-tenths of whom were immigrants or the children of immigrants. The rise of manufacturing during the century profoundly changed the character of the entire state. In 1800 most natives of Massachusetts followed maritime or agricultural pursuits; yet by the middle of the century there was substantial manufacturing throughout the state, even in distant Berkshire County. As the growth of the city and the spread of industrialization was rapidly befouling the countryside, concern developed in Boston for the preservation of the landscape.

In the course of the nineteenth century nearly all the natural features of the hilly, water-ringed Shawmut peninsula, upon which Boston had been settled in 1630, disappeared. Hills were cut down to fill in the coves. By the time there were no more hills left, railroads made it possible to bring gravel from pits miles away on the mainland. The Back Bay of the Charles River was converted from water into land in the course of the years 1857 to 1888, creating a new and handsome residential area. Fortunately in 1875 the city of Boston had the foresight to create a Park Commission, which sought the advice of Frederick Law Olmsted, the landscape architect who was responsible for the design of New York City's Central Park. At that stage of the filling, Commonwealth Avenue, Boston Common, and the wide central boulevard of the new Back Bay led from the Public Garden to the noxious flats of the Muddy River, by which sewage from Brookline drained into the Charles River. Olmsted solved that dilemma brilliantly by a plan that was undertaken in 1881.

By means of skillful drainage and unobtrusive improvement of natural contours, Olmsted converted the course of the Muddy River into a wholesome and decorative park known as the Back Bay Fens, skirted on the east by an avenue called the Fenway which wound off to Brookline, Jamaica Pond, and a new municipal Franklin Park in West Roxbury. Thus the center of Boston and the country to the southwest were linked by a continuous chain of pleasant open spaces that took full advantage of the existing features of the landscape.

Harvard University's professor of horticulture, Charles Sprague Sargent, was at this moment attempting to convert a derelict farm in Jamaica Plain into the Arnold

Arboretum, a place in which he hoped to assemble specimens of every tree and shrub he could find anywhere that might prove hardy in the New England climate. In 1877, he engaged Olmsted to lay out this property, to design roads and paths that would allow a great variety of trees and shrubs to be planted in spots not only where they would seem to be at home, but in which things of a kind would be placed conveniently together for botanical study. This Olmsted accomplished brilliantly, taking full advantage of the varied natural contours of the land. Sargent further conceived the idea of incorporating the Arnold Arboretum into the new park system of the city of Boston. To achieve an agreement between Harvard and the city government seemed as unlikely as bringing peace to Northern Ireland today, but Sargent was not only an energetic scholar but a man of the world, with private means, and a knack for getting things done. By a miracle of town-and-gown cooperation, he persuaded Harvard to deed one hundred and twenty acres of land to the city, which were then leased back to Harvard for one thousand years, at the annual rent of one dollar, on a tax-free basis, with a renewable lease. The city agreed to construct and maintain the driveways shown in Olmsted's plan and to furnish police protection, in return for the admission of the public, between sunrise and sunset, so long as they behaved themselves. This was as sound a business arrangement as could have been worked out in State Street. Ninety-five years later neither party has ever had cause to regret it.

Until his death in 1927, Professor Sargent was constantly adding to the living resources of the Arnold Arboretum. He traveled to many parts of the world in search of trees and shrubs that would flourish in the climate of Jamaica Plain. Even more acquisitions resulted from expeditions to China, Japan, Taiwan, and Korea carried out under Arboretum sponsorship between 1907 and 1922 by the English plant collector and botanist Ernest Henry Wilson. Many of the handsome flowering trees, bushes, and plants that now adorn American parks and gardens are Chinese immigrants, naturalized through the efforts of Professor Sargent, who, once he had found that a specimen could survive here, would pass along seeds or cuttings to nurserymen for commercial propagation and sale.

The work of Frederick Law Olmsted and Professor Sargent made some of their neighbors aware of the need for preserving elements of the landscape outside the jurisdiction of the Boston Park Commission that were soon likely to be obliterated by suburban sprawl. Effective action of lasting consequence began in the eighteen-nineties through the work of the young landscape architect Charles Eliot, son of President Charles William Eliot of Harvard University. After graduation from Harvard in 1882, Charles Eliot entered Olmsted's office as an apprentice, for at this time no university offered formal instruction in landscape architecture. Late in 1885 he went to Europe for a year of travel and study; on his return to Boston in December 1886 he began independent practice.

On February 22, 1890, Charles Eliot wrote a letter to the editor of *Garden and Forest*, entitled "The Waverley Oaks: A Plan for Their Preservation for the People." Pointing out the need for public open spaces within reach of the city of Boston, Eliot wrote:

> Within ten miles of the State House there still remain several bits of scenery which possess uncommon beauty and more than usual refreshing power. Moreover, each of these scenes is, in its way, characteristic of the primitive wilderness of New England, of which, indeed, they are surviving fragments. At Waverley is a steep moraine set with a group of mighty Oaks. At the Upper Falls of the Charles River the stream flows darkly between rocky and broken banks, from which hang rank upon rank of graceful Hemlocks. . . . I shall name no others, though several are well known to all lovers of nature near Boston.

Most of these were in private hands, and Eliot noted that many were in "daily danger of utter destruction." As they were scattered through different towns or along the border lines, Eliot believed that "only an authority which can disregard township limits can properly select and establish the needed reservations."

To achieve this end he proposed

> an incorporated association, composed of citizens of all the Boston towns, and empowered by the State to hold small and well-distributed parcels of land free of

> taxes, just as the Public Library holds books and the Art Museum pictures—for the use and the enjoyment of the public. If an association of this sort were once established, generous men and women would be ready to buy and give into its keeping some of these fine and strongly characterized works of Nature; just as others buy and give to a museum fine works of art.

The analogy was timely, for only twenty years before, in 1870, the Museum of Fine Arts in Boston had, on the instigation of the Boston Athenaeum, Harvard University, and the Massachusetts Institute of Technology, been chartered by the Commonwealth. Since 1876 it had occupied a building in Copley Square, built by private subscription, in which works of art, given by generous individuals, were freely available to all comers. As this had been accomplished entirely from private gifts, and with the blessing but not the financial support of the state, Charles Eliot envisioned the creation of a similar museum without walls—to anticipate a phrase of André Malraux—for the preservation of the natural beauty of landscape.

On March 5, 1890, Eliot outlined his proposal to both Professor Sargent and Charles Mann, president of the Appalachian Mountain Club. The latter organization was active in organizing weekly excursions in the vicinity of Boston to places interesting for their scenery or historical associations. Eliot was a member of its council, where he had made himself useful in respect to the publication of an excellent contour map of the country around Boston. Before the month was out Eliot had drawn up what he called a "Preservation Scheme," which the club's council considered at a meeting on April 2. On this occasion Eliot, Mann, and Roswell B. Lawrence (who in 1886 had published an account of the Middlesex Fells, accompanied by a map) were appointed a committee to call a meeting of interested persons at the Massachusetts Institute of Technology on May 24, 1890.

About one hundred people came from various parts of Massachusetts, while some four hundred letters of support were received from well-wishers who were unable to be present. Letters from Governor John Q. A. Brackett, the poets John Greenleaf Whittier, Oliver Wendell Holmes, and John Boyle O'Reilly, and the historian-horticulturist Francis Parkman were warmly applauded. A distinguished committee was appointed, of which Professor Sargent and Frederick Law Olmsted were members and Charles Eliot secretary, to "promote in such ways as it may seem to it advisable the establishment of a Board of Trustees to be made capable of acquiring and holding, for the benefit of the public, beautiful and historical places in Massachusetts."

To make a long story short, the momentum generated by Charles Eliot's letters of March 5, 1890, was so effective that in less than fifteen months—in May 1891—the Massachusetts legislature passed a bill incorporating the Trustees of Public Reservations, of which he was the first secretary. This was a privately supported body, which, in Eliot's phrase, "did not possess either the money or the authority to snatch real estate out of the hands of anybody." But it trusted that lovers of nature and history would rally to endow it with the care of important sites as lovers of art had endowed the Museum of Fine Arts. The new organization was instrumental, incidentally, in achieving the passage of legislation in 1892 that created the Metropolitan Park Commission, to which Charles Eliot became professional adviser.

The following year, Eliot became a partner in the Olmsted firm, which adopted the name of Olmsted, Olmsted, and Eliot. For four years he was associated with it, not only on work in Boston but with park systems in other parts of the country. A career of seemingly limitless promise was cut short by Eliot's death in 1897 at the age of thirty-six. The record of his life and work is touchingly set forth in a 768-page volume entitled *Charles Eliot Landscape Architect*, published by Houghton Mifflin and Company in 1902. This was prepared by President Charles W. Eliot, who gave no indication of his authorship beyond the dedication:

FOR THE DEAR SON
WHO DIED IN HIS BRIGHT PRIME
FROM THE FATHER

The most enduring memorial to Charles Eliot is the organization whose creation he inspired, for eighty years after his death, the Trustees of Public Reservations (today known simply as the Trustees of Reservations) continues to play an active role in the preservation of the Massachusetts landscape.

Even in its earliest years the influence of this body was far reaching. It was the model upon which the National Trust for Places of Historic Interest and Natural Beauty was organized in Great Britain in 1895. When the Massachusetts Trustees of Reservations were asked to nominate one of their number as a member of the provisional council of the new National Trust, they designated Professor Charles S. Sargent. As the National Trust for Historic Preservation, chartered in 1949 by the Congress of the United States, was inspired by its British predecessor of 1895, it is striking to reflect that Charles Eliot's thought expressed in two letters in 1890 has been an inspiration to historic preservation not only in Great Britain but in the fifty United States.

In 1897, the year of Eliot's death, the Trustees received the gift of fifty acres of Mount Ann, the table of Thompson Mountain in West Gloucester, overlooking all Cape Ann, in memory of Henry Davis Minot. Subsequent additions, one as recent as 1968, have increased Mount Ann Park to eighty-seven acres. In 1934 twelve acres of Halibut Point, the rocky headland that forms the northern tip of Cape Ann, were given to the Trustees. In 1897 the Rocky Narrows in Sherborn, the area mentioned by Eliot in his *Garden and Forest* letter, where the Charles River winds through ledges crowned with hemlock, were acquired. With subsequent additions, the latest of which was made in 1974, this reservation now consists of seventy-seven acres.

Eighty-six years after its incorporation, the Trustees of Reservations is the custodian for sixty-one sites throughout Massachusetts, totaling more than 13,689 acres of seashore and woodlands, river banks, hilltops, headlands, marshes, and wildlife areas, held in fee and open to the public. In addition the Trustees hold conservation restrictions against building upon thirty-five other pieces of land, which insure that 3870 acres will remain in their natural and scenic condition in perpetuity. Thus Charles Eliot's dream has already achieved the protection of 17,559 acres of Massachusetts land. All this has come from private gift. Often individuals who have owned or loved a given site have given or bequeathed it to the Trustees. Once a reservation has been established, neighbors have added adjoining land, or friends have given money that has permitted it to be bought. Thus the acquisition of any site has created a public spirit that has proved to be contagious.

The Trustees of Reservations operate from a house at 224 Adams Street in Milton, from which one looks toward Boston harbor across the ten acres of Governor Hutchinson's Field, a property given to them in 1898 that preserves the view enjoyed in the eighteenth century by a Royal Governor of the Massachusetts Bay. Gordon Abbott, Jr., who has been director since 1967, supervises a year-round staff of 34 full-time employees, scattered throughout the state, that in summer grows to 168 full and part-time people. The operating budget of 1977 was $851,714. Each reservation has a local committee of friendly neighbors that works closely with the professional staff.

A few examples will indicate the way in which the organization has carried out its mission. Among the 61 sites that it owns in fee are the 238 acres of Old Town Hill in Newbury, described so feelingly in the seventeenth century by Judge Sewall. Forty years ago the hill was owned by a farmer, Stephen P. Hale, who loved the land and wanted it preserved. As an old man, he made walking sticks that he gave to people going up the hill. When the day came that it seemed that "Hale's Old Town Hill Public Park" might have to be divided into house lots, the Trustees of Reservations stepped in. Through the generosity of Mrs. George A. Bushee, who summered in Old Town Farm, at the foot of the hill, a reservation was established in 1952, with an endowment. She added another 5 acres in 1966. Sixteen acres of upland and salt marsh from the old Leigh farm bordering the reservation were given in 1973 and 1974 by Professor and Mrs. Elliott Perkins, who had bought the property in 1942 for weekend and summer use.

Adjoining my land in North Andover are the 89 acres of the Stevens-Coolidge Place, a farm bequeathed to the Trustees of Reservations in 1962 by Mrs. John Gardner Coolidge. A mile away is the Weir Hill Reservation with 177 acres of wooded ridges that face the shoreline of Lake Cochichewick, the largest body of water in Essex County and the water supply of the town of North Andover. This reservation was given in 1968 by the estate of Abbot Stevens. Two miles away in the opposite direction in Andover is the 595-acre Charles W. Ward Reservation, which includes the 420-foot Holt

Hill, the highest point in Essex County. In 1940 Mrs. Ward gave and endowed 154 acres of land in memory of her husband. Subsequently other members of the family, as well as Phillips Academy in Andover, have added materially to the acreage.

Chauvinistic residents of Essex County note with pleasure that the Trustees of Reservations own thirteen properties within its limits. But the reservations are scattered widely throughout Massachusetts from the Berkshires to Cape Cod and the Elizabeth Islands—with ten in Norfolk County, six each in Worcester and Berkshire counties, and four each in Plymouth and Hampshire counties. Only Bristol County is not represented in the list. While the Trustees have sought scenery rather than architecture, they have accepted a few houses that have been accompanied by significant land. Among them are three National Historic Landmarks: The Old Manse in Concord, the Mission House in Stockbridge, and the William Cullen Bryant Homestead in Cummington. At Naumkeag in Stockbridge they also preserve the house Stanford White designed for the Honorable Joseph H. Choate. Among the properties of the Trustees are examples of every kind of significant natural landscape, while the 251-acre World's End Reservation at Hingham offers not only dramatic topography but magnificent landscaping, designed in 1890 by Frederick Law Olmsted.

One especially appreciates the work of the Trustees when one compares scenes that they have preserved with similar ones that have been abandoned to the mercy of man and mammon. The 1352-acre Richard T. Crane, Jr. Memorial Reservation at Ipswich consists of a glorious sand beach and dunes, salt marsh, and upland that stretch along the shore of Ipswich Bay for more than four miles. Once one enters the reservation, the mechanized world is exchanged for one of sea, sand, and tranquility. This is because the area was in sympathetic private ownership until 1945 when it was given to the Trustees of Reservations. Early in the nineteenth century Revere Beach and the Saugus marshes must have been equally attractive, but proximity to Boston was their ruination. The narrow-gauge line of the Boston, Revere Beach & Lynn Railroad made the beach easily accessible to the burgeoning population of Boston, which on five occasions increased more than forty percent within a decade. Hotels, amusement parks, and shabby structures began to intrude upon the beach. The Metropolitan Park Commission did its best to cope with the situation after observing conditions on July 12, 1895—a warm Sunday—when 45,000 people visited the beach. By the end of the year, with a million dollars appropriated by the legislature, Revere Beach was "taken" by the Commission for a distance of three miles.

Plans were developed by Olmsted, Olmsted, and Eliot for terraces, shelters, and bathhouses that, in a decent and orderly manner, would take care of the thousands of people who thronged there in summer. Yet outside the area controlled by the Commission, nasty little cottages, with names like "Ishkabibble," proliferated. It is sad that men so often kill the things they love. They rush from the city and create suburban slums in the country, with the added disadvantage of having to spend substantial amounts of time and money to get to and from work. The sight of water, whether the ocean or a modest inland pond, exacerbates the frenzy. One of Miss Sirkis's photographs shows a row of tightly packed identical cottages on a Provincetown beach, stretching endlessly in the manner of a city block.

If visual proof of the value of the work of the Trustees of Reservations is needed, it is only necessary to drive from Boston along Revere Beach, continue to Ipswich, go the length of Argilla Road, get rid of one's car, and walk in the Crane Reservation. Without the work of this devoted organization over the past eighty-six years, and of other groups and individuals inspired by it, there would be far less Massachusetts landscape to enjoy.

The American love affair with the automobile has greatly damaged landscapes everywhere. When people traveled only by train, electric trolley, horse, bicycle, or on foot, the rate of destruction was slower. As automobiles proliferated, public transportation deteriorated. When I came to North Andover in 1936, there were twenty passenger trains a day to Boston; today there are none. Only a few years before we settled there, there had been a railway line to Lawrence and Salem, as well as rural trolleys to other nearby places. As all movement is now over the highway, parking problems have increased in towns as well as cities, with a consequent epidemic of retail shopping centers in regions that only a few years ago were open country. Thus pleasant hay fields, pastures, and market gardens have been black-topped for parking lots. The late Nan

Fairbrother once observed that a parked car, whether Volkswagen or Rolls-Royce, constitutes litter in the landscape.

As the interstate highway system began to change the landscape even in regions remote from cities, Americans began to realize that they had lost control of their surroundings. The words *ecology* and *environment* suddenly became war cries as the prospect of a macadamized continent seemed horrendously near. Marshes and swamps, which had hitherto seemed to many people something to be filled as rapidly as possible, suddenly became precious "wet-lands." Groups were formed to protect many aspects of creation, even the rattlesnake who had hitherto enjoyed only a low popular esteem. Lawyers explored the possibility of scenic and agricultural easements that might protect land from being taxed, as if every plot were the potential site for a factory, shopping center, or condominium. Conservation commissions were organized. Legislation at all levels of government began to be enacted.

Much of this activity was to the good, but some of it slipped beyond the bounds of reason. We are a faddy nation, given to sudden and excessive changes of direction. We long ignore a problem and then suddenly attack with a vigor that, through its excesses, can be counterproductive. The odor of burning leaves was long one of the delightful aspects of a New England autumn; yet I am prohibited from burning mine because of regulations designed to achieve clean air. Most leaves now get trucked to what was once a dump, now elevated to the euphemism of "sanitary land fill," where they do nothing to enrich the soil. To the small number of people who have worked quietly but consistently over decades for the preservation of their surroundings, it sometimes seems that the new breed of vocal ecologists resemble reformed reprobates who have suddenly "got religion."

This new fervor soon reached high levels in the federal government. In 1970, the United States Commissioner of Education, invited to address the American Council of Learned Societies in Washington, gave a fervent after-dinner speech on what he called the "triple E." Professor B. J. Whiting of Harvard University, an eminent Chaucerian who hailed from East Northport, Maine, thus reported the address to the Mediaeval Academy of America, whose delegate he was.

Mr. [James E.] Allen [Jr.] came out strongly against pollution and in favour of "environmental and ecological education. If our communications do not fail us in this crisis, all Americans will to some degree become ecoactivists." Activism cannot start too early and we must begin with the public schools. He said that every school should have access to an outdoor study area where youngsters can learn the interdependence of all the numberless elements of nature. [*Washington Post*, January 24, 1970.] Some of the older delegates who had grown up in rural areas were seen to smile nostalgically and a little wistfully as they remembered outdoor areas where they had first come upon the lessons of nature's numbers, such as that one and one can make three. Other delegates and guests felt that Mr. Allen's remarks were not completely appropriate to so august and learned a gathering, and indeed they did seem directed to teachers of general science in schools for retarded children. The censorious should remember that Mr. Allen is a public servant in one of the more vocal departments [HEW], that he makes many speeches to many and diverse groups and that before he sets out someone supplies him with a paper to deliver. Accidents happen in the best regulated departments and this time someone gave Mr. Allen the wrong speech.

Near Barnstable, Cape Cod.

< Scorton Creek, Cape Cod. ∧ East Dennis, Cape Cod.
∨ View from the fish pier, Chatham.

MS 51 1CC

< Lobster Cove, Cape Ann. ∧ Fisherman and his catch, Gloucester.

< Halibut Point, Cape Ann. ∧∨ The lobster fisherman's equipment, Annisquam, Cape Ann. >> Plum Island.

∧ Sand dunes, Provincetown, Cape Cod. ∨ Water patterns in the sand, Nausett Beach, Cape Cod. > Provincetown.

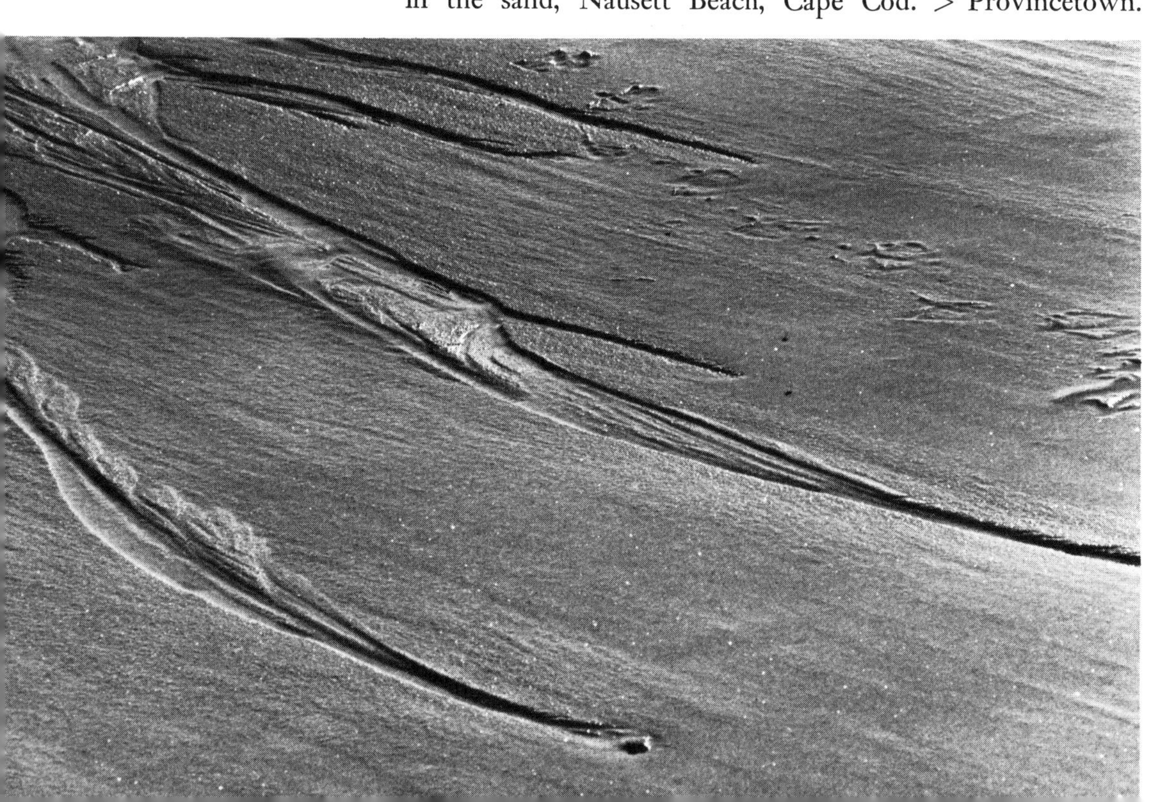

∧ Mussel diggers, Plum Cove, Cape Ann. > *Top*: Bearskin Neck, Rockport. > *Center*: Provincetown, Cape Cod. > *Bottom*: Nantucket.

CIRCUS
CIRCUS
CAFE
LIQUORS
udder
Baby Watson

Nantucket
Pewter
the camera shop

< Quarry, Rockport. ∧ Wingaershaeek Beach, Gloucester. ∨ Divers off Cathedral Rocks, Gloucester. > Gingerbread house in Oak Bluffs, Martha's Vineyard

Preservation of Buildings

The need of doing something to preserve the history of Massachusetts was sensed, and acted upon, a century before Charles Eliot called attention to the landscape. The Massachusetts Historical Society, the first such organization in the United States, was founded during the first term of George Washington's presidency. The Reverend Jeremy Belknap, minister of the Federal Street Church in Boston, author of a *History of New Hampshire*, begun during an earlier pastorate in that state, summoned four friends in August 1790 to discuss the possibility of forming a society for the "collecting, preserving and communicating the Antiquities of America." The Massachusetts Historical Society was formally organized on January 24, 1791. Although it was only incorporated in 1974, it began collecting books and manuscripts immediately after its formation, issuing its first publication in 1792.

As it was organized on the model of a European academy, it has always been a small body, relying on the industry and generosity of its members. Resident membership was originally limited to thirty; although this number was raised to sixty in 1794, to one hundred in 1857, and to one hundred and seventy-five in 1975, it has not increased proportionately to the growth of the population. Membership has been considered a semi-honorary recognition of those who have contributed to Massachusetts history by the gift of manuscript sources, by studying and editing them, or by some other means.

The Frary House, Deerfield, originally built in 1750. A south wing was added in 1760 when the house became a tavern.

The society's resources are, however, freely available to all scholars who have need of them, while its publications, numbered in the hundreds, make those manuscripts available to historians who are far distant from 1154 Boylston Street in Boston.

The second organization of this type to be created in the United States was the New York Historical Society, organized in 1804, while the third was the American Antiquarian Society, founded in Worcester, Massachusetts, in 1812 by the scholar-printer Isaiah Thomas. Like the Massachusetts Historical Society, the American Antiquarian Society is a great research library of American history, concerned with the collection, preservation, and dissemination of source materials. The pattern of these privately supported organizations was soon emulated in other states; by 1864 one had been founded in every state east of the Alleghenies. Their activities in collection and preservation were, however, confined to what could be placed on the shelves of a library or archive. Although portraits to hang on walls and objects suitable for a "cabinet of curiosities" fell within their scope, none of them conceived of *buildings* as historical documents.

Until the middle of the nineteenth century, examples of architecture were treated pragmatically in the United States. They survived if they continued to be useful; if not, they were demolished or fell into ruin. The only surviving seventeenth-century Puritan place of worship in Massachusetts is the Old Ship Meeting House in Hingham. Built in 1681, it was considerably altered and enlarged in the eighteenth century. It continued in active use, however, and in 1930 it was restored in a manner that revealed the structural elements of the original building.

Such a survival would only be possible in a town that grew at a moderate rate. The First Church of Boston, established in 1630, and the Second Church of 1660 replaced their meeting houses repeatedly, even moving to quite different parts of the town to follow their congregations. The oldest surviving place of worship in Boston is Christ Church, Salem Street, built in 1723 for the second Anglican parish in the town. Although this has been in continuous use for more than two hundred and fifty years, the preservation of the building was not due to its religious vitality. In the nineteenth century, as the North End ceased to be a fashionable residential district, the parishioners of Christ Church dwindled, for the new residents of the region were successively Irish Catholics, Jews, and finally Italian Catholics. Through the accident of signal lanterns having been hung in the church's belfry on the night of April 18, 1775, to warn Paul Revere of the route to be followed by British troops marching to Lexington and Concord, Christ Church became part of American historical mythology. Henry Wadsworth Longfellow's poem "Paul Revere's Ride" nicknamed the building Old North Church, by which name it has been known to generations of American schoolchildren. Like some of the Christopher Wren churches in the city of London, it acquired a respect out of all proportion to its religious usefulness. Early in this century the Right Reverend William Lawrence, Bishop of Massachusetts, applied artificial respiration by becoming the unpaid Vicar of Christ Church and persuading some of his solvent friends living in other parts of Boston to transfer their membership to Christ Church in order to provide funds for the upkeep of the parish.

Although Christ Church has become chiefly a place of historical pilgrimage to the shrine of Paul Revere's signal lanterns, Episcopal services are held there. When Queen Elizabeth II visited Boston on July 11, 1976, her first act after coming ashore from the yacht *Britannia* was to attend morning service in Christ Church, at which the Duke of Edinburgh read one of the lessons.

King's Chapel, begun in 1750 as the second building of the first Anglican parish in Boston, has also survived in continuous use through the accident of having become, during the American Revolution, the first Unitarian church in Massachusetts. Although Charles Bulfinch designed four churches in Boston, only one of them exists today. The New North in Hanover Street, designed in 1802 for a Unitarian society, suffered within a few decades the same loss of supporters as its Episcopal neighbor, Christ Church. When the end came in 1862, the building gained a new lease on life as St. Stephen's Roman Catholic Church, which it is today. But with the shifts of population that occurred in the nineteenth century, Bulfinch's other three churches were demolished as their congregations moved elsewhere. The Catholic Church (later Cathedral) of the

Holy Cross, designed in 1800, came down in 1862; the Unitarian Federal Street Church of 1809 went in 1859; and the New South Church of 1814 in 1868. Although these demolitions represented a major architectural loss to the city, nobody thought twice about them. The buildings were no longer needed; so down they came.

The notion of preserving buildings in the United States sprang from a pious desire to perpetuate scenes that George Washington had known in his lifetime. In 1850 the New York Legislature appropriated $8391.02 to preserve the Hasbrouck House in Newburgh, which had served as Washington's headquarters during the last two years of the Revolution. Three years later Miss Ann Pamela Cunningham of South Carolina began an effort to purchase his home, Mount Vernon, from its owner, John A. Washington, who had set the high price of $200,000 upon the house and its surrounding 200 acres of land. From 1846 on, frequent petitions to Congress to buy the place for the nation had produced no result. The rumor in 1853 that the plantation was to be sold to developers as the site for a hotel, spurred Miss Cunningham to send out an anonymous appeal to the women of the South to attempt the preservation of Washington's home. Through the Mount Vernon Ladies' Association that she created, the place was saved by the dauntless efforts of private citizens, mostly women.

In 1859, the heirs of John Hancock offered his house on Beacon Hill, next to the Massachusetts State House, to the Commonwealth of Massachusetts for $100,000, a price that was somewhat below the commercial value of the land. Although the legislature originally thought the house would make an appropriate governor's mansion, the state procrastinated so long that the heirs demolished the building in 1863. The loud cries of public protest over the destruction were remembered a few years later when the Third Church in Boston—known as the Old South—wished to abandon its 1729 meeting house at the corner of Washington and Milk Streets.

From the church's point of view, the proposal was perfectly rational. The region had been given over to business. The congregation lived in other parts of the city, and the land owned by the church had acquired a commercial value that could never have been anticipated by the generous parishioners who had given it in the last third of the seventeenth century. In 1869 the Old South bought lots in the newly filled Back Bay, at the northwest corner of Dartmouth and Boylston Streets, and built upon them an Italian Gothic building, dedicated in 1875, since known by the contradictory name of the New Old South Church. The Old South Meeting House stood on land worth more than a third of a million dollars. If this could be realized, the sale would cover the cost of the move and the new building, which was near the homes of the congregation.

To Bostonians who remembered the destruction of the Hancock House, the demolition of the Old South represented a loss of something intimately concerned with origins of the American Revolution, the centennial of which was approaching. As it had been the scene of numerous political meetings in the decade leading up to that conflict, of which the most renowned were those that culminated in the Boston Tea Party of December 16, 1773, the building had acquired resounding historical associations in no way connected with its primary function as a Congregational church. The congregation had no objection to its preservation, as long as somebody else footed the bill and they got their money. In the literal sense their attitude was reasonable, for the memory of the Revolution had little to do with the saving of souls, which they considered to be their business.

In 1872 the church attempted to sell the meeting house to the Massachusetts Historical Society, which had neither the funds to enter an inflated real estate market, nor, indeed, the desire to do so. The society's chief aim was, and still is, the acquisition and publication of manuscript sources of American history, rather than acquisition of historic buildings for exhibition. This effort having failed, the church turned to the alternative of selling the site for commercial purposes. After protracted court litigation, in 1876 it was determined to tear down the meeting house in preparation for such a sale.

The building was sold at auction on June 8, 1876, for $1350, subject to removal within sixty days, on the theory that if it were pulled down rapidly enough there would be nothing left to argue about. We have seen in recent years all too many examples of this type of logic by bulldozer. Just as the work was beginning, however, George W. Simmons, a dealer in ready-made clothing, stepped in and bought a seven-day stay of demolition. A mass meeting was called in the building on the fourteenth, at which Wendell Phillips delivered a resounding address in which he declared that "the saving of this landmark is the best monument you can erect to the men of the Revolution." The fight was on, in earnest. A committee was formed to solicit contributions, and several thousand dollars subscribed on the spot.

When twenty Boston ladies bought the building for $3500, its preservation was assured, for, no matter what happened to the land, the meeting house could, if necessary, be moved to another site. On September 15, 1876, the church agreed to sell the land for the then enormous sum of $400,000. The citizens' committee made a down payment of over $75,000 that had been raised in previous weeks, while the New England Mutual Life Insurance Company took a $225,000 mortgage. By a dramatic contribution of the last $100,000, Mrs. Augustus Hemenway assured the success of the project. As at Mount Vernon, determined and resourceful ladies carried the day, even though the sum involved was twice what had been demanded for Washington's home. Thus was the Old South Meeting House preserved as the first instance in Boston where respect for the historical heritage of the city triumphed over considerations of profit, expediency, laziness, and vulgar convenience. With this success, historic preservation in the United States moved into its urban phase.

While the Commonwealth of Massachusetts soon incorporated the Old South Association in Boston to hold the meeting house as a historic site, it never appropriated any funds to assist in that purpose. The mortgage was eventually amortized by a great variety of popular fund-raising enterprises over a number of years. Once saved, the Old South Meeting House was opened to visitors, not only with exhibitions connected with the building and the Revolution, but with popular lectures and publications in American history. In the course of a century, however, Bostonians have come to value the Old South quite as much for the architectural grace that it lends to this part of the city as for the associative values with the American Revolution. On both these grounds the Old South Meeting House was eligible for inclusion in the Boston National Historical Park, created by an Act of Congress on October 1, 1974. Upon the signing on January 12,

1977, of a cooperative agreement, the Old South Association in Boston began to receive substantial assistance from the National Park Service in the operation and maintenance of this National Historic Landmark. After more than a century of private fund-raising for the purchase and maintenance of the meeting house, this federal assistance was welcome.

The preservation of the Old South Meeting House spurred the city of Boston into the restoration of the Old State House, two blocks east on Washington Street at the head of State Street. This brick building, more precisely called the Second Boston Town House, was constructed soon after a fire in 1711 had destroyed the wooden Town House that had stood on the site since 1657. Until the Revolution this second structure served the needs not only of town and county but of the royal government of the province of Massachusetts Bay. Within its walls some of the fiery speeches of James Otis and Samuel Adams had been delivered; from its east balcony the Declaration of Independence had first been read in Boston on July 18, 1776. It served later as the Massachusetts State House until 1798, and as the City Hall from 1830 to 1862. Thereafter it was ignominiously rented as private offices and was so covered with signs and generally disfigured that in 1875 it was nearly torn down. But as the associations of the building were similar to those of the Old South Meeting House, the success of that campaign saved the Old State House. The City Council in 1881 authorized a thorough restoration, completed at public expense the following year at the cost of $35,000. The Bostonian Society, a new organization dedicated to the history of the city, was installed in the building to maintain a local historic museum. When Queen Elizabeth II visited Boston on July 11, 1976, she was officially received at the Old State House, appearing on the balcony from which—two centuries before, less seven days—the Declaration denouncing her ancestor and predecessor, King George III, had been read. Later in the day she visited Faneuil Hall, which the city had in 1898 renovated and fireproofed—once again because of its Revolutionary associations—and had recently titivated because of the Bicentennial.

The impetus to historic preservation provided in Massachusetts by the saving of the Old South Meeting House led to extraordinary activity by a wide variety of groups and individuals. One man, however, had a fruitful vision in regard to buildings—a vision akin to the perceptions of Charles Eliot concerning the landscape. This was another old-line Bostonian, William Sumner Appleton of the Harvard class of 1896. He was born in 1874 at 39 Beacon Street, a fine Beacon Hill house now preserved by the Women's City Club. He was not an intellectual genius, although a pleasant, sociable character. His eyes were weak, and his health poor; his early *pro forma* attempt to go into business did not prosper. He could live, nevertheless, for he was a grandson of a great Boston textile manufacturer and banker, Nathan Appleton. Upon the death of his father in 1903, Sumner Appleton inherited in trust a comfortable competence, which provided him an income, without access to or responsibility for the capital. He never married, and until his mid-thirties he pottered about Boston, making an extra man at dinner, with interludes of travel.

Almost by accident, Sumner Appleton became interested in historic preservation. John Phillips Reynolds, Jr. (1863–1920), a great-grandson of Paul Revere, bought in 1905 a house in North Square in Boston which Revere had owned from 1770 to 1800. The North End having long been an overcrowded slum, the house had fallen upon hard days. Reynolds, who bought it out of family sentiment, wished to insure its preservation as an historical landmark; to that end he asked three friends to organize a movement to raise the money to accomplish this purpose. As the youngest and least busy of the three, Appleton was expected to do most of the leg-work. This gave him an occupation, which he embraced with enthusiasm.

The Committee solicited funds from Revere descendants, from D.A.R. chapters, and from other patriotic organizations throughout the country to such purpose that in May 1907 the newly incorporated Paul Revere Memorial Association took title to the house. Restoration having been undertaken according to plans of the architect Joseph Everett Chandler, the Paul Revere House was formally opened to the public on April 18, 1908. In the course of this effort, Sumner Appleton found his *métier*. Thereafter he looked at other properties associated with the American Revolution to see what could be preserved.

The week before Christmas 1909 he went on three occasions to Lexington. The Jonathan Harrington House on the Lexington Common particularly moved him. Its owner, mortally wounded on April 19, 1775, had dragged himself home, only to die at the feet of his wife, as she opened the door to meet him. This story so touched Sumner Appleton that "it seemed as though a house having such associations should be safeguarded against all alterations." From that moment on December 22, 1909, he felt that "my life's work seemed to be cut out for me."

Appleton moved decisively. Three days after Christmas he was talking with Charles Knowles Bolton, my predecessor at the Boston Athenaeum, about founding a Society for the Preservation of New England Antiquities. He persuaded Bolton to become president, choosing for himself the less conspicuous post of corresponding secretary. By the time of an incorporation meeting on April 23, 1910, he had recruited seventeen friends as members, at an annual fee of ten dollars. In May he sent out the first *Bulletin* of the new society in which he put his case vigorously. On the cover was a photograph of the John Hancock House, destroyed in 1863, with the caption: "The fate of this house has become a classic in the annals of vandalism." Inside Appleton wrote: "Our New England Antiquities are fast diminishing because no society has made their preservation its exclusive object. That is the reason for the formation of this Society." With increasing population and prosperity, the New England scene was fast changing. Unless prompt action were taken, many significant buildings would soon disappear. The existing activities of historical and patriotic societies, which were mostly concerned with single houses, coped with only a fraction of the threats.

"The situation," he stated, "requires aggressive action by a large and strong society, which shall cover the whole field and act instantly wherever needed to lead in the preservation of noteworthy buildings and historic sites." What was new in Appleton's manifesto was the concern with *preserving* buildings, by any means possible, rather than exhibiting them for inspirational purposes. With Mount Vernon, the Old South Meeting House, the Old State House, and the Paul Revere House, the emphasis had been associative rather than architectural. They were saved because of great men who had lived in them or noble events that had taken place within their walls. The aim was to *exhibit* them, like relics of saints, so that some of their value might rub off on the visitors. In Lexington, Sumner Appleton had been moved by the memory of Jonathan Harrington dying on the doorstep of a still existing house; yet by the time he proclaimed the mission of the S.P.N.E.A. he had come to a new purpose, for he continued: "It is proposed to preserve the most interesting of these buildings by obtaining control of them through gift, purchase or otherwise, and then to restore them, and *finally to let them to tenants* under wise restriction, unless local conditions suggest some other treatment."

As a criterion for action, Sumner Appleton brought two new ideas into historic preservation: the validity of architectural beauty or uniqueness (unrelated to historical association), and the idea of preserving buildings for continued use rather than for exhibition. The second notion, of keeping buildings in current use (with adequate safeguards against damaging change) as a part of continuing life—rather than isolating them as objects of inspirational and antiquarian veneration and wonder—opened the way to great advances in preservation during the next six decades. There is a limit to the number of museums that can be afforded; there is almost no limit to the number of imaginative, useful ways that can be found to preserve the essential qualities of good, old buildings.

With a table, a couple of chairs, and a typewriter, Sumner Appleton established the Society for the Preservation of New England Antiquities in a modest upstairs office in a downtown Boston building. His title of Corresponding Secretary was descriptive, for he personally wrote innumerable letters seeking members, answering inquiries, and giving advice in current problems, in addition to editing the society's *Bulletin*. His financial resources were his personal income and what he could beg from friends and relatives. Having found a cause that inspired him, he proved a persistent and effective beggar. In 1912 a full-time stenographer joined him, but the previous year he had succeeded in buying the seventeenth-century Swett-Ilsley House in Newburyport. By the spring of 1915 the society had 1500 members and owned four houses. The next year it acquired title to the house at Cambridge and Lynde Streets in Boston, designed by Charles Bulfinch in 1796 for Harrison Gray Otis. Appleton moved the headquarters of the society there in the spring of 1917, where it still is, sixty years later.

Until his death in 1947 Sumner Appleton worked incessantly for the society that he created. His contemporaries constantly marveled at his energy, and at what he accomplished on a shoestring. In the sixty-seven years since the foundation of the society, he and his successors, Bertram Kimball Little and Abbott Lowell Cummings, have acquired by gift or purchase fifty-nine properties in New England, as well as assets for their maintenance in excess of five million dollars. Some of the properties are regularly open to visitors, others are preserved through private occupancy, but all are safeguarded for the future.

Although the Society for the Preservation of New England Antiquities has been the great rallying point, innumerable buildings of historic and architectural importance have been saved through the efforts of local historical groups and of organizations created to assure the safety of some particular monument. In 1962 I pointed out in Chapter XV of my *Independent Historical Societies* the extraordinary preoccupation with history that is shown in Essex County, Massachusetts. The Essex Institute, a county historical society organized in 1848 through the amalgamation of earlier groups of 1821 and 1833, possesses an extraordinary library, manuscript collection, and museum, in addition to several Salem historic houses of great distinction. Yet at that time, twenty-three out of the thirty-four towns of Essex County had local historical societies of their own. I calculated then that the county had a historical society for every 11,095 acres of dry land. As one or two have been created since, the acreage would be correspondingly lower today. The Ipswich Historical Society's John Whipple House of 1640, the North Andover Historical Society's early eighteenth-century Parson Barnard House, and the Marblehead Historical Society's Jeremiah Lee Mansion of 1768 are excellent examples of buildings preserved through such organizations.

The Isaac Royall House in Medford and the Wayside Inn in Sudbury are pictured by Miss Sirkis. The former was rescued early in this century by a local group before the Society for the Preservation of New England Antiquities was organized. Sixty years ago, when my mother took me to see it, it was sparsely furnished, chiefly with contributions from the local D.A.R. chapter. Today, thanks to the diligence of the Royall House Association, it is admirably restored. As my father's mother had been a native of Sudbury, as a child I saw the Wayside Inn on various occasions. Then it was still a working country hostelry. Railroads had eliminated its usefulness as a stopping place for coaches on the post road, but guests still came to the scene of Longfellow's *Tales of a Wayside Inn*. In the twenties, it was bought by Henry Ford, who had fallen victim to a sentimental nostalgia for the scenes of his youth, which led him to take up square dancing and promote the McGuffey-type education of children. Ford placed the house in the care of a small group of Boston trustees, who still maintain it as a working inn, with due regard to its architectural integrity.

With the growth of Boston in the nineteenth century, adjacent towns were annexed to the city. The land of eighteenth-century farms and country estates was subdivided into lots on city streets. In Roxbury, for example, the country seat of the colonial governor, William Shirley, still precariously survives—thanks to the devoted efforts of the Shirley-Eustis House Association—but in a crowded slum. In Cambridge several fine Tory Row houses of the same period have had a happier fate. Although they have lost the greater part of their original land, through the creation of new streets, they are in a good residential district, beloved of the Harvard faculty. Some are still privately occupied by single families; one is the headquarters of the Cambridge Historical Society. "Elmwood," long the home of the poet James Russell Lowell, is the official residence of the President of Harvard University, and Craigie House—Washington's headquarters during the Revolution, later the home of the poet Henry Wadsworth Longfellow—is cared for by the National Park Service.

A little farther out in Waltham, two large country seats have preserved a decent approximation of their original surroundings in spite of suburban and industrial encroachment. "The Vale," a late eighteenth-century property of the Lyman family, is now maintained by the Society for the Preservation of New England Antiquities, while the nearby "Gore Place," the noble Regency seat of Governor Christopher Gore, is cared for by a society organized for that express and sole purpose. But for every country estate that is so preserved, many others have remained intact only through their conversion into schools, colleges, convents, or some other type of institution.

When I first came to North Andover in 1936, the hill behind my house was surmounted by a yellow wooden approximation of a French château, built for the Sutton family, who were local mill owners. The house has been demolished and the property subdivided. The red brick house of another mill owner, Nathaniel Stevens, still stands in its original surroundings on Osgood Hill, as it has been given to Boston University for a conference center. Around Lake Cochichewick were several large properties that have been converted to new uses. The Tyson place is now a Methodist conference center called Rolling Ridge. Richard S. Russell gave his estate to Brooks School, which he was instrumental in creating. Brooks School has used it sympathetically. The Kunhardt place for some years was used by the Jesuit order as a retreat house, Campion Hall. That having been closed, the future of the house and land is now uncertain.

At the other end of the state, at Lenox in Berkshire County, many large estates became schools, not all of which have survived. Foxhollow School for a number of years owned and used sympathetically "The Mount," Edith Wharton's country house. With the closing of the school in 1976, the future of that National Historic Landmark is in doubt. "Tanglewood," another Lenox country house, allied to the memory of Nathaniel Hawthorne, has an assured future. It has become the home of the Boston Symphony Orchestra's Berkshire Music Festival. During the summer months music lovers throng to "Tanglewood," which has become a New England institution.

Many fine houses in Boston have been preserved by adaptive use. Nearly all Boston clubs and a number of learned societies are housed in this way. Other houses, converted to apartments or offices, have kept their facades and, at best, some of their internal features. Historic Boston Incorporated, organized in 1960, rescued the Old Corner Book

Store at the corner of Washington and School Streets. This house, built soon after a fire of 1711, diagonally across from the Old South Meeting House, has had its façade restored and its interior remodeled for the use of the *Boston Globe*, the Liberty Bank and Trust Company, and other tenants. Thus it provides a congenial neighbor for the Old South Meeting House, besides paying taxes to the city. A few years later the old City Hall, a few yards up School Street, achieved a new lease on life through the imagination of Roger S. Webb's Architectural Heritage group. It now houses the best French restaurant in Boston, a branch of the First National Bank, numerous lawyers, and other tenants. These are but a few instances of the application of Sumner Appleton's ideas.

As the rate of change accelerated in the years following World War II, it became apparent that the preservationist must think not of single buildings but of entire areas. In 1955 the Massachusetts legislature passed acts establishing historic districts on Beacon Hill in Boston and in Nantucket, which placed architectural controls upon the exterior appearance of buildings within an entire area. This was a logical extension of a United States Supreme Court decision of 1954 (*Berman* v. *Parker*) which ruled that a city has as much right to be beautiful as it has to be safe and clean. The Beacon Hill district has subsequently been enlarged, and architectural controls have also been placed upon the Back Bay. Numerous historic districts in other cities and towns have been created under enabling legislation of the state.

The establishment of a Massachusetts Historical Commission in the sixties and a Boston Landmarks Commission in the seventies has involved the state and city governments increasingly in matters of historic preservation, while the National Park Service is playing a new role in Massachusetts. The Park Service's first urban project in Massachusetts was the Salem Maritime National Historic Site—so designated in 1938—which preserves Derby Wharf; the Old Custom-House, at which Nathaniel Hawthorne once worked; and the adjoining Richard Derby House, illustrated in this book.

The Minute Man National Historic Park was established in 1959 to attempt to rescue, in a region of creeping urbanization, what could be preserved of a natural setting of the battle road from Lexington to Concord, which marked the opening of the American Revolution. I have earlier noted how, at the approach of the Bicentennial, the Boston National Historical Park was created, in which the Park Service works—through cooperative agreements with older organizations, such as the Old South Association—to help in the maintenance of buildings associated with the American Revolution. Through the National Park Service and the Massachusetts Historical Commission, federal matching funds have become increasingly available to privately supported preservation efforts in Massachusetts.

I rejoice finally that in 1976 through the efforts of Mayor Kevin H. White and Robert T. Kenney, then head of the Boston Redevelopment Authority, Quincy Market and the adjacent granite-faced warehouses on North and South Market Streets, completed in 1826 by Mayor Josiah Quincy, were restored to the uses for which they were originally intended. This noble composition, designed by Alexander Parris, as an early instance of urban redevelopment, is now restored on the exterior to its original propriety and clearly has a long life ahead of it.

From the Buckman Tavern, Lexington.

In the Isaac Royall House, Medford.

< Salem. ∧ The Derby House (1792), Salem.

Door handle and sewing basket from the Derby House, Salem.

< The battlefield at Concord. ∧ The Parson Capen House (1683), Topsfield.
∨ An interior view of the Abraham Browne House (1698), Watertown.

∧ Front door, Rebecca Nurse House (1678). > Old North Bridge, Concord.

∧ Old Ship Meeting House (1681), Hingham. > The Paul Revere House (1676), Boston.

∨ Beacon Hill. > Louisburg Square, Beacon Hill.

< New Government Center and Old Faneuil Hall (background), Boston. ∨ Copley Square.

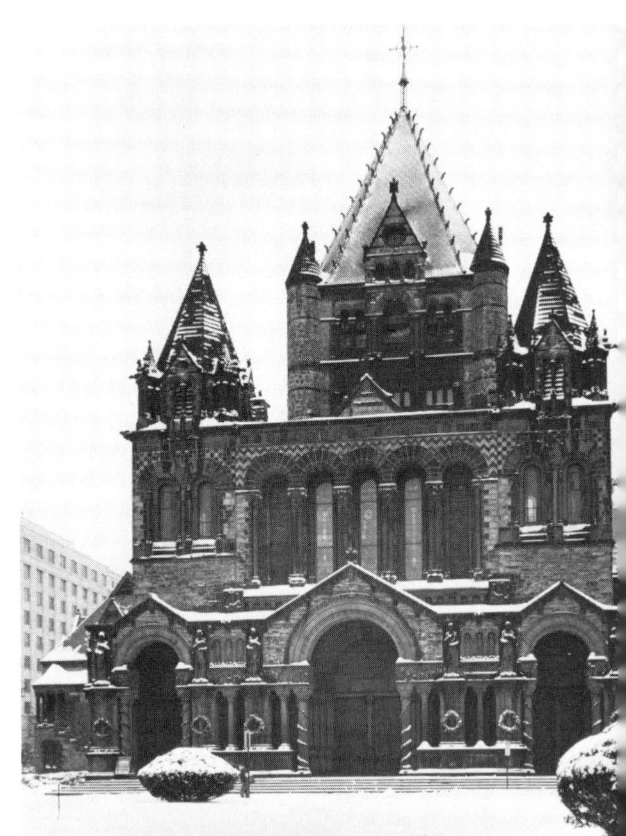

<< Faneuil Hall (1742).

∧ Government Center.

< Trinity Church (1877).

> The old Hancock building reflected in the new, as seen from Longfellow Bridge.

∧ Prudential Building.
> Reflection of Trinity Church in the Hancock Building.

< Along Commonwealth Avenue. ∧ Acorn Street, Boston.

Mills in Lowell (*left*) and Lawrence.

THE NEW KIMBELL
APOTHECARY HALL
GALLUP • DICKEY
INSURANCE AGENCY INC.
RIC

The Edifice Complex

From time out of mind small boys have sniggeringly compared the size and condition of their sexual organs, or vied to determine whose could throw the best stream the greatest distance. Such contests we call childish; yet grown and even distinguished men behave the same way when their minds become affected by the "edifice complex." Presidents of banks, insurance companies, great corporations, and universities suffer from this mental disorder as acutely as the scruffier types of promoters. The desire is for a larger erection than one's neighbor's. As the complex is widespread, the embodiment of such phallic fantasies disfigures cities on every continent.

In a world of walled towns, towers were first defensive. From their heights, watchmen could give early warning of the approach of an enemy, upon whose heads the defenders might rain missiles. Within cities, Christian bell towers and Islamic minarets helped summon the faithful to prayer. By the nineteenth century many defensive towers had vanished, leaving the spires of churches and mosques as the chief accents in an otherwise tolerably uniform skyline. Buildings stayed low, for there was a limit to the number of stairs that people were willing to climb in the course of daily life.

With the introduction of elevators buildings began to rise. The Equitable Life Assurance Society building in New York, constructed in 1868–1870, reached 130 feet. As engineers developed new uses of iron and steel, it became possible to reach greater heights without the need of unreasonably massive foundations and bearing walls. This

North Adams.

upward movement caused the word "skyscraper"—originally the sky-sail of an eighteenth-century sailing vessel—to be applied to a tall building. While the *Oxford English Dictionary* recorded no instance of this usage before 1891, Mathews' *A Dictionary of Americanisms* cited this instance in the *Century Magazine* for September 1883: "The Georgia man . . . writes to the 'American Architect' to say that the American mind requires 'skyscrapers.' "

The first instance, however, where an immensely tall structure dominated a skyline was not in America but in France. In 1889, when the French Government sought a dramatic symbol for the Paris exposition commemorating the centennial of the French Revolution, the bridge builder Eiffel conceived a wrought-iron tower of open lattice work that rose to the height of 984 feet, far beyond the pyramids of Egypt or the dome of St. Peter's in Rome. The Eiffel Tower became the most conspicuous structure in Paris. For forty years it was the tallest in the world. Moreover, through the use of new techniques, it was achieved in a matter of months, at not unreasonable cost. Such a feat of engineering put ideas in many heads. It was only a step to think of filling such a skeleton with windows, and inserting floors—to achieve, in place of an observation tower, a gigantic office building.

In the first half of the twentieth century, the skyscraper became the trademark of New York City. As Manhattan Island was long and narrow and completely surrounded by rivers, space was at a premium. There was nowhere to go except up. For a time architects tried to clothe the new monsters in historic styles to give the illusion of continuity with an earlier world. Thus the 1909 tower of the Metropolitan Life Insurance Building recalled the campanile of Venice, while the 779-foot Woolworth Building of 1913 was encased in Gothic decoration that suggested the appellation "cathedral of commerce." The concentration of tall buildings at the lower end of Manhattan Island produced a dramatic effect that was particularly striking when seen from ships entering the harbor from Europe. It was, however, only with the Chrysler Building of 1929–1930 that the height of the Eiffel Tower was exceeded.

The mood in Boston was different. While New Yorkers were seeking the skies,

Bostonians cherished a ninety-foot-height limit which left the gold dome of the State House and church steeples as the only accents in the profile of the city. When forward-looking developers in 1898 undertook to build the Hotel Westminster in St. James Avenue on the edge of Copley Square they ignored the restriction. The Museum of Fine Arts, then located next door on the present site of the Copley-Plaza Hotel, sought to confirm the limits of future buildings by legislation, which was duly passed. The museum then sought an injunction restraining the builders of the Westminster from proceeding with their plans. While hearings dragged on, the roof of the offending hotel was completed. In September 1898 the Attorney General of Massachusetts required the demolition of any part of the Westminster that exceeded the ninety-foot limit. This decision was enforced to such purpose that the upper stories were removed.

For a decade and a half thereafter, the Boston skyline remained unchanged. Our first modest skyscraper sprouted in 1915 through circumstances that no one could have anticipated. The granite Doric temple of 1838 that served as the Boston Custom-House having been outgrown, federal funds were available only for its enlargement, but not for its replacement on another site. As there was no adjacent vacant land, the architects Peabody and Stearns substituted for the temple's low dome an Italian campanile of an office building. Nothing could be done to prevent it, for as the Custom-House was federal property, it was exempt from the municipal height limit. It remained for some thirty years the only conspicuous tower of the Boston skyline.

While various buildings in the business district crept up to 125 feet, the residential Back Bay remained a region of five-story houses and churches until 1927, when the twelve-story Ritz-Carlton Hotel was, by exception, permitted to violate the Arlington Street skyline. Once an exception is made, it becomes increasingly difficult to prevent others. Moreover, soon after the First World War, business began to creep toward the Back Bay. To the south of Boylston Street, a new center for insurance companies developed in a large area left vacant after the abandonment of the Park Square terminal of the Boston and Providence Railroad. In 1947, the John Hancock Mutual Life Insurance Company, located on Clarendon Street between St. James Avenue and Stuart Street, added a tower, fronting on Berkeley Street, which for some years made the building New England's tallest. On its completion, *Newsweek* claimed that "it does for Boston just what the Empire State Building does for New York." Although the scale was smaller, the idea was similar.

As land was filled during the nineteenth century to link the original Shawmut peninsula with the Roxbury and Brookline mainland, the principal thoroughfares of the new South End and Back Bay bore little relation to each other. Those of the South End were extensions of the older Washington and Tremont Streets, running off to the southwest. Those of the Back Bay ran due west from the center of the Public Garden. Consequently there was between the two sections a triangular no-man's land, long occupied by the yards of the Boston and Albany Railroad. After the Second World War, the Prudential Insurance Company bought these train yards, which became the site of the largest twentieth-century development in Boston.

The central feature of the Prudential Center, which began to be used in 1965, is a fifty-two-story tower, flanked by the twenty-nine-story Sheraton Boston Hotel, three twenty-six-story apartment buildings, and, at lower heights, the city's John B. Hynes Memorial Auditorium, and a number of retail stores. This then became a windy, self-contained world of its own, where one could work or shop, live temporarily or permanently. Its architecture is undistinguished, but it is a vast improvement over the swamp and train yards that it replaced, which had been an eyesore for a century. It is a mercy when so large a development can be built without demolishing anything of superior quality. Moreover, this development bridges the triangular chasm that long separated the Back Bay and the South End, thus helping to unify the city.

The Prudential tower can be seen from a considerable distance; the view from its observation deck offers a panorama of nearly half of Massachusetts. It is the lower buildings of the center that clutter the landscape. When one stands in Copley Square, looking west, they make a Chinese wall behind the Boston Public Library. The lesson is that one tall building is often less obstrusive than two half the height or four of a quarter the elevation. This can clearly be appreciated from some of the photographs in this book.

The word *high-rise* first afflicted my ears in the nineteen fifties, when it came into common use by architects and developers. In the post-war years there was a mania everywhere, even in Boston, for tinkering with zoning and building codes to allow tall buildings here, there, and everywhere. Post-war euphoria, abetted by federal urban renewal funds, caused many developers, greedy for gain, to devastate American cities. The Boston Redevelopment Authority, established in 1957, began the following year to clear a forty-eight-acre tract in the West End, which brutally displaced people, disrupted existing neighborhoods, and destroyed attractive buildings, only to create in the center of the city an area that long resembled a vast approximation of a battlefield. Eventually, apartment towers, far beyond the purses of the former residents of the West End, and two high-rise office buildings, rose to occupy the cleared land.

The West End was demolished before most Bostonians were aware of what was going on, through the process of "urban renewal," not only in Boston but in many cities throughout the United States. The indignation aroused by this effort was so great that Mayor John F. Collins early in his administration determined that federal funds available for urban renewal must be used in a more imaginative way that would enhance rather than obliterate the unique character of the city. Consequently in 1960 he appointed as Chairman of the Boston Redevelopment Authority the Right Reverend Monsignor Francis J. Lally, respected editor of the archdiocesan newspaper, *The Pilot*, and brought to Boston as Development Administrator Edward J. Logue, a man of outstanding competence, experience, and energy. In the seven years that he spent in Boston, Ed Logue emphasized renewal rather than wholesale rebuilding and demolition. Early in his tenure he pointed out: "Renewal and rehabilitation do not guarantee beauty. It is entirely possible to rebuild Boston in an unimaginative, unattractive way that will make people wonder whether the new is in fact better than the old. This can be avoided with sufficient forethought and courage. It is the function of distinguished architecture and imaginative civic design to see that beauty is the hallmark of the renewed city. Beauty once flourished in Boston. It must again."

By extraordinary skill, Logue meshed together the aspirations of the city, state, and federal governments and won the willingness of the financial and business community to cooperate in his proposals. He foresaw the danger that enthusiasm over the new Prudential Center might cause banks and law firms to rush west in the city, as the insurance companies had already done, thus abandoning the old State Street axis. This had happened in New York where, with the construction of new skyscrapers in midtown Manhattan, the old homogeneity of doing certain kinds of business in the vicinity of Wall Street at the lower tip of the island was being lost. The Hotel Westminster, on the edge of Copley Square, had already been demonlished to make room for a new federal office building. If enthusiastic developers began promoting high-rise buildings on any piece of land that they bought, chaos was just around the corner.

As the City Hall, built during the Civil War, was long outgrown, Logue visualized its replacement as the key to a new Government Center in Scollay Square, a central area that had for some years been the site of burlesque houses, shooting galleries, and other establishments much patronized by servicemen on leave. Most of the buildings could reasonably be spared. This new center would provide conveniently adjacent space for badly needed state and federal office buildings, as well as new private ones that would reinforce State Street. Logue's first step was to engage I. M. Pei and Associates of New York City to design the project in broad terms, delineating sites for the various uses and establishing controls of height and bulk that would achieve pleasing relationships between the buildings.

The keystone of Pei's plan was the new City Hall, set in a broad, open space. Because of its proximity to the historic Faneuil Hall, it was conceived as a relatively low building covering considerable ground. He suggested low, curving, private office buildings for the east and west sides of the new square, and a new federal office building on the north, while on the south the existing Sears Crescent of Cornhill was retained as a link between the new and the old. Pei's specifications were used as the basis for a national competition for the new City Hall, a competition sponsored by the Boston Society of Architects and won by a group of relatively young and unknown architects, Gerhard M. Kallman, Noel M. McKinnell, and Edward F. Knowles of New York City. Theirs was the best design submitted, and it was promptly executed. The new City Hall is a huge, low building, with handsome and convenient interior spaces, well suited to the various aspects of city government. To me it has always seemed as fine a building for its time and place as Boston has ever produced.

Pei's plan established a subtle balance between low buildings and taller ones. To the north of the City Hall the John Fitzgerald Kennedy Federal Building consists of two twenty-six-story towers fronting on Cambridge Street, bridged by two long, low rectangular extensions that help enclose the new City Hall Plaza. Beyond them, in the region that was once Bowdoin Square, were placed the new state office buildings. On the southwest corner of the Government Center the plan called for a privately financed office tower that would provide a link with State Street. Considerable squabbling ensued over the development of this site.

While this was in progress, British investors conjured up by the architect Frederick A. Stahl began construction of a thirty-four-story office building at 225 Franklin Street, only a few blocks away from the middle reaches of State Street. The State Street Bank and Trust Company rented the lower floors for their headquarters and gave their name to the building. The opening of the State Street Bank Building in the spring of 1966 made it clear that the financial center of Boston would remain downtown, rather than move west to the edge of the Back Bay. It also set off a chain reaction of new construction for other banks. The edifice complex was never more clearly demonstrated. If one bank gave its name to a glittering new tower, the others had to follow suit.

The real estate firm of Cabot, Cabot and Forbes built a forty-story tower at 28 State Street—the site designated for a tower in Pei's Government Center Plan. The New England Merchants National Bank, which had already moved part of its operations to the Prudential Center, became the prime tenant here and gave its name to the building. Cabot, Cabot and Forbes then undertook a second forty-story tower on Washington Street at the head of State, to which the Boston Safe Deposit and Trust Company moved its main office. The First National Bank then built itself a thirty-seven-story tower at Franklin and Federal Streets, while the National Shawmut Bank, not to be outdone, constructed its new tower on the site at Milk and Federal Streets vacated by the removal of the First National. This game of musical chairs very considerably changed the skyline of downtown Boston. The Custom-House of 1915 acquired so many neighbors that it became almost inconspicuous.

The practice of "Monkey see, monkey do" sometimes leads men to plan more tall buildings than a city needs or its citizens want. A developer casts his eye upon a site. To assemble the lots needed, he may pay prices so high that he can retrieve his investment only by the construction of a very large building. Having optimistically cleared the site, he may then encounter strong opposition to carrying out his plan or may discover that the market is not as rosy as he thought. The completion of two towers at the head of State Street led Cabot, Cabot and Forbes to plan a third at 60 State Street. The buildings there had hardly been demolished when a time-consuming controversy developed. The relationship of the new building to Government Center introduced complications; the fact that it would, as originally planned, overshadow Faneuil Hall brought historic preservationists into the problem. For a number of years there was a yawning hole in the ground at 60 State Street. The design was modified. At the moment of writing, the building is now visible among its tall neighbors, but there has been a recession, and it is not yet clear whose name it will bear, or who the tenants will be.

As tall buildings have proliferated, many people have become aware that they are not entirely comfortable things to live with. The wind whistles around their bases; they cast great shadows; often they have little architectural distinction. As preservationists and environmentalists have not only become more articulate but have become armed with effective legal weapons, development projects are often subjected to time-consuming scrutiny. For several years the Park Plaza project, in the vicinity of Park Square, has been the subject of endless hearings and reviews, in which citizens have presented their concern about the effect of unduly tall buildings upon the adjacent Public Garden. Construction is not yet in sight, but if it ever begins, the buildings will probably rise less high than the proponents of the project originally wished.

The tallest building in Boston is, ironically, one of the least obtrusive, because of the skill of its architects. The John Hancock Mutual Life Insurance Company announced in November 1967 its plan to build upon the site of the Hotel Westminster a 790-foot, sixty-story tower. The architects, I. M. Pei and his Boston-born associate, Henry N. Cobb, made every effort to provide upon a limited site the two million feet of floor space required by the company, without overwhelming Copley Square. Their solution was an eight-story base that would reinforce the building's relation to its near neighbors, from which would rise a slender fifty-two-story tower in the shape of a rhomboid. To make the building as light as possible, it was enclosed in anodized aluminum and mirror-glass, which reflect the hourly and seasonal changes of light. As the rhomboid tower was placed obliquely, the building unobtrusively edges into, rather than dominates, Copley Square. It is less in evidence than some of the lower blocks of the Prudential Center, which are a greater distance away.

Unanticipated problems with its mirrored glass delayed the occupation of the Hancock tower until 1976. Now that it is completed, its windows offer a constantly changing series of reflections of clouds, sky, and neighboring structures, depending upon the point from which one looks at it. Miss Sirkis shows two very different views of it. A distant one (from the Longfellow Bridge) shows the new tower reflecting the outline of the 1947 Hancock building. A near view, taken in St. James Avenue, presents the reflection in the windows of the eight-story base of H. H. Richardson's Trinity Church, directly across the road.

The constrained limits of Manhattan Island provided a logical reason for building skyscrapers. The sad aspect of the edifice complex is that people delight in flaunting their contemporaneity by high-rise erections in places where there is not the necessity. This is a universal affliction today. In Massachusetts it has spread beyond Boston, as Miss Sirkis's photographs of Worcester, Springfield, and the campus of the University of Massachusetts at Amherst demonstrate. One of the saddest pictures in the book is the view of a tall building in Worcester, from whose windows the occupants look down upon a nasty landscape of buses, automobiles, gas stations, and highway signs that could be, but ought not to be, anywhere.

DUSTY'S TAX

Mural and shopping center,
Springfield.

∧ Country road, Tyringham. > View from Stafford Hill, Cheshire.

Pond near Bow Wow Road,
Sheffield.

Old Sturbridge.

Tanglewood Music Festival, Lenox.

∧ The Green, Brookfield. > City Hall, Worcester.

NATIONAL BANK

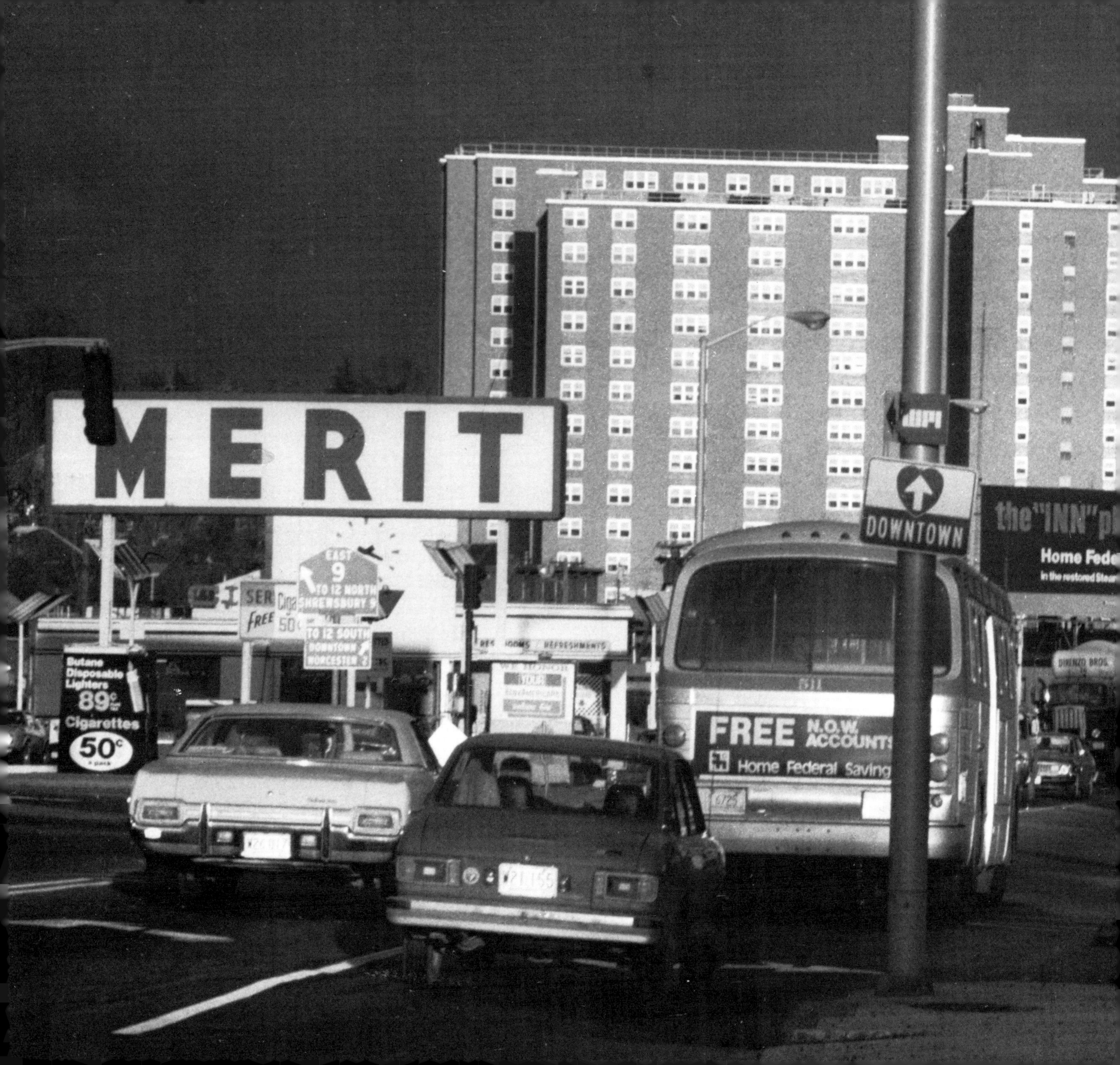
MERIT
EAST
9
TO 12 NORTH
TO 12 SOUTH
DOWNTOWN
WORCESTER
Butane
Disposable
Lighters
89¢
Cigarettes
50¢
a pack
REST ROOMS / REFRESHMENTS
DOWNTOWN
the "INN" pl
Home Fede
FREE N.O.W.
ACCOUNTS
Home Federal Saving
DIRENZO BROS.

Worcester.

Snowmobile tracks, Deerfield.

< Brewster mudflats.

∨ Wellesley girls' rowing team.

On the campuses of Wellesley College (*left*) and the University of Massachusetts at Amherst.

Along the Money Brook Trail, Mt. Greylock, the Berkshire Mountains.

Snowscape, the Berkshires.

< Plowed field, Deerfield. ∧ Pontoosac Lake, Springfield. ∨ Butternut Ski area, Great Barrington.

Near Stockbridge.
>> View of the Berkshires from the summit of Mt. Whitcomb.

Afterword

Most of the photographs in this book present a pleasing picture of Massachusetts. But because much of the state *is* attractive, so many tourists swarm into it during the summer that they create in many coastal towns an approximation of Coney Island or a shoddy Florida resort. Year-round residents of Cape Ann, Cape Cod, and the Elizabeth Islands eagerly await the arrival of Labor Day, for thereafter life returns to normal for the next eight months. This summer-tourist phase of Massachusetts life is epitomized in the photographs of Rockport, Provincetown, and Nantucket on page 49.

One summer Saturday afternoon a few years ago I went to Rockport to attend a funeral. Although I arrived in ample time, so many tourists were thronging to the shops on Bearskin Neck that by the time I had succeeded in parking my car half a mile away and walked back to the church, the funeral was over and the corpse was being carried out. Although it is a long drive to the tip of Cape Cod, Provincetown can be reached by road, while Nantucket and Martha's Vineyard are accessible only by ship and plane. Yet so many day-trippers rush to the Elizabeth Islands that residents who wish to take their cars to or from the mainland at Woods Hole have to reserve space weeks in advance.

In November 1966 the Massachusetts Department of Commerce and Development asked me to address a conference at Northeastern University devoted to the study of recreation, tourism, and vacationing in eastern Massachusetts. In my remarks I suggested that the tourist trade is one of the offerings of the Devil, and that any region that encourages it, and is satisfied with the results, has lost its soul beyond recovery. The trade benefits those who rent rooms, operate busses, and sell fried clams, gasoline, and knick-knacks, but it is a burden to people who try to preserve the historical resources of the region, and a nuisance to those who live in the vicinity. I applied to those who fatten on the tourist trade the words of the prophet Jeremiah: "But when ye entered, ye defiled my land, and made mine heritage an abomination."

Although this was not what the conference wished to hear, the sponsors with great honesty printed my remarks in full in their 418-page report of the proceedings. In an article, "Tourist, Stay Home!", in the *Saturday Evening Post* of August 12, 1967, I thus described the address:

> This statement raised a lively hubbub. A public official described listening to my address as a "traumatic experience." A Boston newspaper reporter suggested that I be placed in the stocks on Boston Common, adding that "the stocks would be justified because Dr. Whitehill smokes a pipe and has a bushy beard, and if the spectacle could be open to public inspection it should serve as quite a tourist attraction in itself."

With this background, I anticipated the Bicentennial of the American Revolution with singularly little enthusiasm. In Boston, well before the bicentennial of the opening of hostilities on April 19, 1775, there were anniversaries of the so-called "Boston Massacre" of 1770 and the Tea Party of 1773. As the Revolution lasted until 1783, and as promoters of the tourist trade gloatingly anticipated super-colossal waves of visitors, the future seemed depressing indeed. The one bright side of the "energy crisis" was that the shortage and high price of gasoline might foil the dreams of the promotionally minded. It certainly reduced them, for the summers of 1975 and 1976 were not conspicuously worse than their predecessors.

In the spring of 1976 my spirits rose, for with the evacuation of Boston by the British on March 17, 1776, we had run out of local anniversaries to celebrate. As the theater of military operations moved to the southwest, New York, Philadelphia, and other places were free to do what they liked; we were through! Then in early July

1976 the visits of the Tall Ships and of Queen Elizabeth II aroused tremendous popular enthusiasm. Anything else would have seemed an anticlimax. With the arrival of 1977 and a new President, the word *Bicentennial* ceased to be heard. Although no one said so formally, it appeared that we had been celebrating the Bicentennial not of the American Revolution but of the Declaration of Independence. So by common consent nearly everyone stopped the flag-waving and went back to work. It was a great relief.

Every year thousands of men and women come to study in the schools and colleges of Massachusetts. Many of them like the state so much that they stay, in spite of a climate that offers extreme contrasts more rapidly than most. All phases of Massachusetts life—universities, hospitals, laboratories, industries, and professions—are constantly enriched by these converts, who blend imperceptibly into the local scene. Such recruits are highly welcome; it is only the tripping gawkers of the tourist trade who rush through the state, dressed as if for a beach, scattering beer cans behind them, that we can do without.

COLLEGE OF MARIN LIBRARY
3 2555 00007954 6